Canada

THE ROUGH GUIDE

There are more than one hundred Rough Guide titles
covering destinations from Amsterdam to Zimbabwe

Forthcoming titles include
Central America • Chile
Indonesia • Japan • New Orleans

Rough Guide Reference Series
Classical Music • European Football • The Internet • Jazz
Opera • Reggae • Rock Music • World Music

Rough Guide Phrasebooks
Czech • Egyptian Arabic • French • German • Greek • Hindi & Urdu
Hungarian • Indonesian • Italian • Japanese • Mandarin Chinese
Mexican Spanish • Polish • Portuguese • Russian • Spanish
Swahili • Thai • Turkish • Vietnamese

Rough Guides on the Internet
http://www.roughguides.com

ROUGH GUIDE CREDITS

Text editor: Kieran Falconer
Series editor: Mark Ellingham
Editorial: Martin Dunford, Jonathan Buckley, Jo Mead, Samantha Cook, Kate Berens, Amanda Tomlin, Ann-Marie Shaw, Paul Gray, Sarah Dallas, Chris Schüler, Helena Smith, Caroline Osborne, Judith Bamber, Olivia Eccleshall, Orla Duane, Ruth Blackmore (UK); Andrew Rosenberg (US)
Production: Susanne Hillen, Andy Hilliard, Judy Pang, Link Hall, Nicola Williamson, Helen Ostick, James Morris

Cartography: Melissa Flack, Maxine Burke, Nichola Goodliffe
Picture research: Eleanor Hill
Online editors: Alan Spicer, Kate Hands (UK); Geronimo Madrid (US)
Marketing & Publicity: Richard Trillo, Simon Carloss, Niki Smith (UK); Jean-Marie Kelly, SoRelle Braun (US)
Finance: John Fisher, Celia Crowley, Neeta Mistry
Administration: Tania Hummel, Alexander Mark Rogers

ACKNOWLEDGEMENTS

The **editor** would like to thank the monumental patience of production: Susanne (for not shouting), Judy, Link, Helen, Nicola and James; Eleanor Hill; Maxine and Nichola who finally got their maps, and Nikky Twyman for tireless proofreading. Special thanks go to Bunkins, Skippy and Possum for smoothing over the occasional kerfuffle, Joe Green for his incredible contribution to the quality of life, and finally, Steve and Kate Galbraith.

Tim: James and Vicky Ballantyne, Tim Burford, Jane Wigham at Air Canada, Ruth Roberts at Tourism British Columbia (London), Amanda Newby at Travel Alberta (in the UK) and Greyhound (UK).

Phil: A special thanks to the tourist departments of New Brunswick, Nova Scotia, PEI, Ontario and Toronto, without whose splendid assistance I would have been struggling. Particular thanks also to Liz Blakeborough, Tim Burford, Paula Harris, Diane Helinski, Carol Horne and Valerie Kidney, as well as John Hamilton and Helen Lovekin for their trenchant comments on Toronto. Love to Cathy and Emma Rees, and Mum.

Tania: Marta Reyes in Ottawa, Isabel Martin and her colleagues at Tourisme Québec, Robin at Call of the Wild and Hemingways. Special congratulations to Kieran Falconer for his understanding and amusing debut as editor. Plus love and thanks to my best and beautiful friends – Finny Smith, Charlotte Bouchier, Kamin and Saba Sams.

Kirk: John and Jeffrey King, Rochelle Yanofsky, Pat Matheson, Colette Fontaine at Travel Manitoba, Nadine Howard at Tourism Saskatchewan, Cathy Anderson and Charlotte Jewczyk at Newfoundland Dept of Tourism, Culture and Recreation, Jean-Hugues Detcheverry at L'Agence Regionale du Tourisme St-Pierre et Miquelon, Nim Singh at the Canadian Tourism Commission (London), Curt Koethler at Tourism Regina, Vickie Clarke at Tourism Saskatoon, Bernadette Walsh at Dept of Economic Development and Tourism (City of St John's), Cathy Crotty at Destination Labrodor, staff at the Happy Valley–Goose Bay Visitor Centre.

PUBLISHING INFORMATION

This third edition published May 1998 by Rough Guides Ltd, 62–70 Shorts Gardens, London WC2H 9AB. Reprinted in December 1998. Previous editions 1992, 1995. Distributed by the Penguin Group:
Penguin Books Ltd, 27 Wrights Lane, London W8 5TZ
Penguin Books USA Inc., 375 Hudson Street, New York 10014, USA
Penguin Books Australia Ltd, 487 Maroondah Highway, PO Box 257, Ringwood, Victoria 3134, Australia
Penguin Books Canada Ltd, 10 Alcorn Avenue, Toronto, Ontario, Canada M4V 1E4
Penguin Books (NZ) Ltd, 182–190 Wairau Road, Auckland 10, New Zealand
Typeset in Linotron Univers and Century Old Style to an original design by Andrew Oliver.
Printed in England by Clays Ltd, St Ives PLC
Illustrations in Part One and Part Three by Edward Briant.

Illustrations on p.1 & p.861 by Henry Iles
© Tim Jepson, Phil Lee and Tania Smith 1998
No part of this book may be reproduced in any form without permission from the publisher except for the quotation of brief passages in reviews.
944pp - Includes index
A catalogue record for this book is available from the British Library
ISBN 1-85828-311-6